# A Walk Thru the Life of

# ELIJAH

## Standing Strong for Truth

Walk Thru the Bible

**BakerBooks**

*a division of Baker Publishing Group*
Grand Rapids, Michigan

© 2010 by Walk Thru the Bible

Published by Baker Books
a division of Baker Publishing Group
P.O. Box 6287, Grand Rapids, MI 49516-6287
www.bakerbooks.com

Printed in the United States of America

Library of Congress Cataloging-in-Publication Data
A walk thru the life of Elijah : standing strong for truth / Walk Thru the Bible.
   p.  cm.
Includes bibliographical references (p.   ).
ISBN 978-0-8010-7176-8 (pbk.)
1. Elijah (Biblical prophet) 2. Bible. O.T. Kings—Textbooks. I. Walk Thru the Bible (Educational ministry)
BS580.E4W28 2010
222′.5092—dc22                                 2009046945

Scripture is taken from the HOLY BIBLE, NEW INTERNATIONAL VERSION®. NIV®. Copyright © 1973, 1978, 1984 by International Bible Society. Used by permission of Zondervan. All rights reserved.

10   11   12   13   14   15   16       7  6  5  4  3  2  1

# Contents

# Introduction

It seemed like a gift to humanity, a harmless pleasure meant to benefit all who partook of it. Sure, there were a few uptight naysayers who warned that tobacco might be dangerous, but they had no proof. Besides, the world is full of people who over-react, who can't loosen up and enjoy life. If you listen to all of them, you'll lose your mind. Most warnings from hypersensitive people turn out to be totally false.

For years, smoking was considered benign. Ever since native Americans gave tobacco to Columbus, there had always been a few detractors, but their voices went unheeded. And though suspicion of harmful side effects grew throughout the early 1900s, the general public wasn't concerned enough to curtail the habit. In fact, smoking's popularity grew; nearly half of American adults, particularly men, enjoyed cigarettes in the mid-1940s, including the vast majority of doctors. The habit was so entrenched that few people gave much thought to the seeming overreactions of detractors. The American Medical Association even argued in 1948 that evidence pointed more toward the health benefits of smoking, such as stress relief, than toward any physical ailments resulting from it. Huge cultural trends aren't swayed by arguments that there "might" be a problem.

At the time of the Old Testament kings, few people were really bothered by Israel's idolatry either. Altars had been set up all over the territory of the northern ten tribes, and people freely worshiped Baal and Asherah and whomever else they wanted to worship. Did the God of Moses have a problem with that? Not as far as anyone could tell. Sure, a few prophets and priests here and there may have spoken up, but they were a distinct and easily ignored minority. Rain still fell in the right seasons, crops still grew in the fields, the building programs of kings signaled progress on every front—everyone seemed to prosper. Hardly anyone recognized that a deadly cancer had long been developing in the spiritual life of the nation. Even those with a nagging suspicion that there might be a problem weren't concerned enough to do anything about it.

That's where Elijah enters the stage of Israel's history. He is a warning signal, a voice in the wilderness, alerting God's people to their deadly practices. His message wasn't very popular—no one who successfully declares a three-year drought on his own people gets high marks in public opinion polls—and it didn't seem like the kind of message a loving God would speak. But it was necessary. A loving God doesn't just sit by and watch cancer spread among his chosen people. He sends a wake-up call in the form of Elijah.

The message of Elijah—and of most of the prophets, for that matter—is that God often disciplines his people harshly, not primarily because of his anger but because of his love. But the prophet who speaks of such discipline carries a very politically incorrect message. God's judgment on a nation can become a thorny theological issue. When his scriptural promises to bless those who love and obey him and to withhold his blessing from those who don't are actually carried out, lots of questions arise. Are the blessings and curses of the Old Testament valid today? Where does grace fit into the equation? Why would God let the innocent suffer from the same conditions he imposes on the unrighteous?

The Bible doesn't thoroughly answer such questions. It doesn't even attempt to address them in 1–2 Kings, books written to chronicle how Israel experienced both the blessings and curses foretold in Deuteronomy. No, the purpose there is to report the highs and lows of God's people in the Promised Land—and ultimately to explain why God used another nation as a tool of his judgment to overthrow them. Long ago through Moses, God had given Israel very specific instructions and told them what consequences to expect both for obeying them and not obeying them. He would bless them if they kept his ways and worshiped him alone, and he would curse them if they didn't. The historical accounts of the Old Testament in general, and more specifically Elijah's story, are progress reports on their faithfulness.

## The Elijah Enigma

Elijah seems to appear out of nowhere. No genealogy introduces him, he has no established reputation, and even today no one knows where his hometown of Tishbe was. He steps into Scripture mysteriously and disappears from it even more mysteriously.

One other figure visits the biblical story as a similar enigma. In Genesis 14, after Abraham pursues and overtakes an invading coalition of kings, a mysterious priestly figure named Melchizedek appears—no genealogy or hometown, no prior reputation, no explanation. Abraham shares a sacred meal with him, offers him a tenth of the spoils of war, and receives his blessing. But unlike Melchizedek, who came to bless Abraham, Elijah has a confrontational mission. He came to warn Israel and, eventually, to curse King Ahab.

Unlike many of the later prophets, Elijah didn't write his prophecies. He simply emerged from the landscape, distinguished himself from the communities of prophets that functioned in kings' courts and around religious centers, and spoke brief but powerful decrees of what God would do in response to Israel's idolatry and injustices. The skeletal details of his life presented in 1–2 Kings only add to the mystery of who he was. All we know is that he lived in the ninth century BC during the reigns of Ahab and Ahaziah. An unusual, colorful character, his ministry lends itself to speculation.

Even after his departure from Israel's history, Elijah's personality hovers over its collective hopes. He still serves as a prototypical prophet—rugged and extreme, the epitome of countercultural zeal. In Hebrew thought, Moses represents the law and Elijah represents the prophets. He shows up in the writings of later prophets and in the ministry of Jesus, who pointed to Elijah as an example of God's heart for the Gentiles (see Luke 4:25–26). And the expectations of his continuing ministry didn't end with the New Testament, as we'll see. He remains a dominant figure in the Jewish past and present.

## How to Use This Guide

The discussion guides in this series are intended to create a link between past and present, between the cultural and historical context of the Bible and real life as we experience it today. By putting ourselves as closely into biblical situations as possible, we can begin to understand how God interacted with his people in the past and, therefore, how he interacts with us today. The information in this book makes ancient Scripture relevant to twenty-first-century life as God means for us to live it.

The questions in this book are geared to do what a discussion guide should do: provoke discussion. You won't see obvious "right" answers to most of these questions. That's because biblical characters had to wrestle with deep spiritual issues and didn't have easy, black-and-white answers handed to them. They discovered God's will as he led them and revealed himself to them—the same process we go through today, though we have the added help of their experiences to inform us. Biblical characters experienced God in complex situations, and so do we. By portraying those situations realistically, we learn how to apply the Bible to our own lives. One of the best ways to do that is through in-depth discussion with other believers.

The discussion questions within each session are designed to elicit every participant's input, regardless of his or her level of preparation. Obviously, the more group members prepare by reading the biblical text and the background information in the study guide, the more they will get out of it. But even in busy weeks that afford no preparation time, everyone will be able to participate in a meaningful way.

The discussion questions also allow your group quite a bit of latitude. Some groups prefer to briefly discuss the questions in order to cover as many as possible, while others focus only on one or two of them in order to have more in-depth conversations. Since this study is designed for flexibility, feel free to adapt it according to the personality and needs of your group.

Each session ends with a hypothetical situation that relates to the passage of the week. Discussion questions are provided, but group members may also want to consider role-playing the scenario or setting up a two-team debate over one or two of the questions. These exercises often cultivate insights that wouldn't come out of a typical discussion.

Regardless of how you use this material, the biblical text will always be the ultimate authority. Your discussions may take you to many places and cover many issues, but they will have the greatest impact when they begin and end with God's Word itself. And never forget that the Spirit who inspired the Word is in on the discussion too. May he guide it—and you—wherever he wishes.

# Far from God

## BACKGROUND

It was one of life's strange mysteries, an eerie echo from the deep, dark past. Out of the blue, with no warning from the gods, an ancient curse was tragically fulfilled. One of the founding fathers had uttered this jinx, but no one really believed it anymore. The fathers had uttered plenty of predictions that never came true. This was just one legend among many.

Until now. This prediction was startlingly accurate. One day, the entrepreneur who had been building a city on the long-neglected ruins of Jericho suddenly lost his oldest son in the building of the foundations. Soon after, his youngest died in the building of the gates—exactly according to Yehoshua's legendary words.

Why? What capricious deity was responsible for such a travesty? This noble kingdom had easily matured beyond its forebears' predictions. None of the other ancient curses had been fulfilled. The founding fathers had promised drought if Elohim's primitive commandments were abandoned, but everyone knew this threat was simply to manipulate the people. The old superstitions were obviously no longer relevant. Baal had been worshiped freely for years, and he always brought his rain in season. The rider of the clouds was plentiful with his storms. Serving Baal had served Israel well. So why would this singular curse from age-old writings come true?

Such was the spiritual climate in Israel after its split from Judah following Solomon's death. Jeroboam, the first northern king after the split, had set up altars in Bethel and Gilgal where golden calves could be worshiped. He was making a major statement against the southern kingdom and its recently built temple, departing from the religion of David's dynasty. Six kings later, Ahab and his queen made Baal worship the state religion by constructing an altar in Samaria and building worship centers for Baal's consort, Asherah, around the country. Many Israelites worshiped both Baal and Yahweh without any sense of contradiction. Yahweh was the absentee God above all other gods, but Baal was the practical deity who brought rains and harvests. Like adherents of many religions today—including Christianity—they accepted a hybrid or compromised version of the pure faith once given to them and called it "progress."

We see throughout Scripture, and specifically as we examine Elijah's life, that God is constantly calling his people back to the beginning. That's why orthodox Jews still rigorously study the Torah, and Christian pastors and theologians appeal to the authority of the Gospels and Acts. When God has spoken and

## GODS AND GODDESSES

Ahab built a temple dedicated to Baal, a storm god who, in Canaanite culture, was responsible for bringing rains and harvests. In the eyes of true devotees, allegiance to him could make a huge difference in the semiarid climate: if Baal was pleased, the entire country would have food and water; if not, the people would suffer hunger and drought. Devotion to Baal was expressed in various ways throughout Canaanite history, including self-laceration and, at times, ritual prostitution. Ahab seems to have been influenced heavily by both his father, Omri, and his wife, Jezebel. As the Phoenician king's daughter, Jezebel may have been a high priestess of the Phoenician Baal, a god of war and death. Together, she and Ahab set up a system of worship that exalted the Canaanite Baal and his consort, Asherah, who was worshiped openly at poles set up throughout the countryside in her honor. The king/priest and queen/priestess possibly saw themselves as an image of this divine couple.

later generations have gotten off course, it's important to return to the roots—to revelation in its purest form. In Elijah's day, the kings of Israel had seriously departed from their ancient roots in the exodus and the words of Moses. God sent a prophet to turn them back.

**Detours: 1 Kings 16:29–34**

When Solomon died, his son was advised to take it easy on the people. After all, the great king had almost enslaved them to get the temple and his palace built. But Rehoboam vowed an even harsher reign than that of his father. The result? The northern ten tribes of Israel seceded and formed their own kingdom. Jeroboam established alternate worship sites, replete with golden calves. The tribes of Judah and Benjamin could

13

keep Jerusalem and its shrine to Yahweh. The northern people of Israel would worship however they saw fit.

Omri was the sixth king in the north, and he "sinned more than all those before him" (16:25). He built Samaria as the capital city and allied his kingdom with the Phoenicians—a relationship sealed with the marriage of the crown prince Ahab to the Phoenician princess Jezebel. When Ahab became king, he continued in his father's idolatry. In fact, like his father, he too "did more evil in the eyes of the LORD than any of those before him" (16:30). He and Jezebel made Baal worship the kingdom's official religion.

That probably seemed innocuous enough to most Israelites, who assimilated lesser gods into their belief in a single supreme deity. Few Israelites would have seen themselves as having abandoned the religion of Yahweh, even though they hardly knew his commandments and broke them without much sense of disobedience or guilt. They may have committed to have no other gods *before* him, but their conscience didn't seem to dictate against having plenty of gods *beneath* him. They were nominal

## ISRAEL'S KINGS

Jeroboam led the revolt against Solomon's son, Rehoboam, and became the first king of the northern ten tribes, referred to as Israel. The southern kingdom retained the name of its largest tribe, Judah. During the era of the divided kingdom, nineteen kings ruled in Israel before the Assyrian conquest (Ahab was the seventh); and twenty kings ruled in Judah before it was carried off to captivity in Babylon. Of the twenty kings of Judah, eight were commended for at least partially following the ways of the Lord. But of the nineteen kings of the north, none were commended. All nineteen allowed open idolatry and "did evil in the sight of the LORD" (16:25).

believers in the God of the exodus without adhering to his laws. Over time, they became comfortable with a hybrid faith—and with Yahweh fading further and further into the background. The temple of Baal and the poles erected in honor of Asherah, Baal's feminine counterpart, didn't seem to bother them.

## Discuss

- Do you see any parallels between Israel's departure from true faith and Western Christianity today? If so, what are they?

_____

_____

_____

_____

## Consequences: Deuteronomy 11:13–17; Joshua 6:26

Roughly six decades had passed since Jeroboam split from Judah and built altars to golden calves in the northern kingdom (1 Kings 12). But Yahweh didn't seem to mind; in fact, Israel was prospering as much as any other country. The kings who succeeded Jeroboam walked in his ways, ignoring God's desire for exclusive worship at a designated place and cultivating instead a pluralistic society with a range of deities to choose from. God's chosen people, at least in the northern kingdom of Israel, had forgotten what it meant to be chosen.

But some of them remembered. Some who had not yet bowed to Baal recalled God's words in Deuteronomy 11—the promise of rain and harvests if God's people worshiped him alone and the warning of drought and famine if they didn't. Still, it had been six decades, and the fields remained fertile. That's why

15

perhaps it was a shock when Joshua's ancient curse came true. Centuries before, when the walls of Jericho had fallen, Joshua proclaimed that whoever tried to rebuild the city would lose his firstborn son in the foundation and his youngest son in the gates. The reconstruction would come at a heavy price. And he was right. A builder named Hiel found out the hard way that with God, old words are not forgotten words.

**Discuss**

- In what ways do we tend to compromise our worship of the one true God? What "idols" do you think people wrestle with most?

  _____

  _____

  _____

  _____

- Do you think the promises and warnings of Deuteronomy—abundance for those who worship God and scarcity for those who don't—apply at all to us today, either literally or figuratively? If so, in what ways?

  _____

  _____

  _____

  _____

## A CASE STUDY

_Imagine:_ You live in a society steeped in its religious traditions and confident that it is special in the eyes of God. Its scriptures are in every bookstore and on most coffee tables but are hardly ever read. Its worship services are attended regularly but rarely seem to impact daily life. While nearly all people assume their own piety, you've noticed a huge discrepancy between what they claim as truth and how they actually live. In fact, their "sacred" beliefs and traditions are violated daily without regret. And, given your strong belief in the God of the sacred past, you're frightened by how he might respond.

- How would you address the situation? Would you make a public but extremely unpopular stand, or would you simply worship in your own way and let others do the same? Why?
- In what ways would you expect God to correct the false assumptions this society has about him?
- What discrepancies do you see between your society and its sacred traditions? How do you think God might want to address those discrepancies? How should you?

# War of the Gods

## 1 KINGS 17

William Tyndale was once told by a clergyman that translating the Bible into the common language was an insignificant task. It would be better for people to know the pope's laws than God's, the minister warned. But Tyndale was zealous about his conviction that ordinary people should be able to read God's Word for themselves. He translated both testaments into common English. And it eventually cost him his life.

That's what often happens when someone stands up as the conscience of the culture and insists on going against the flow. Martin Luther nearly lost his life in the aftermath of his ninety-five theses that challenged church doctrine as being unbiblical. William Wilberforce ruffled more than a few feathers and risked his political career in his campaign against the British slave trade. Countless voices have been cut off because they saw evil and injustice and wouldn't let it slide. A prophetic stance is confrontational and polarizing—and usually very dangerous.

Such was the case with Elijah. He saw an entire society falling away from its divine purpose and a king and queen who enthusiastically supported the shift. The gap between God's plan and Ahab's policies was frighteningly vast. Someone had to say something, and surely God would support the one who did. The Lord's own purposes were at stake. The divine voice could not be silent any longer.

God prompted Elijah to speak. We don't know exactly how that happened—whether it was the voice of conviction, an audible voice from heaven, or something in between. We do know that Elijah was emphatic about God's purposes. We may not find ourselves proclaiming predictions with the same degree of certainty that Elijah did, but God does fill us with his truth

## A WIDOW'S FAITH

Jesus once observed some rich people giving extravagant gifts into the temple treasury and used the opportunity to teach his disciples a lesson about faith. He pointed out a poor widow who contributed two very small coins and lauded her for her extravagance. After all, she had given all she had out of her poverty. The others had given out of their wealth (Luke 21:1–4). Jesus's Jewish listeners would have immediately recognized the parallel to the widow of Zarephath. Out of her poverty, she gave Elijah, God's prophet, the last flour and oil she had. It was an act of trust that was rewarded with God's abundant supply. Her resources never ran out, illustrating a principle found throughout Scripture: those who sow seeds of faith into God's kingdom will find the faithfulness of God in response.

and a sense of conviction. Like Elijah, we have a role in challenging the status quo, especially when the status quo is at cross purposes with the kingdom of God. Those who know God are called to represent him to the world.

## A Lone Voice: 1 Kings 17:1

With no introduction, the prophet appears in the name of Yahweh and declares war against Baal. His name is his message—Elijah means "Yahweh is God"—and his challenge is aimed at Baal's alleged strength: rain. Only one deity can rule the heavens and govern the weather, and it isn't a Canaanite storm god. It's the God who long ago warned that he would shut up the skies if Israel departed from him. Now is the time for Yahweh to prove who is Lord.

Is Elijah following direct orders from God, or is he declaring his own convictions based on a scriptural promise? Was it the present Spirit or the ancient Word that prompted him? The text doesn't say; the prophet simply speaks. He tells Ahab that rain will not come until he gives the word at an unspecified time—in "a few years." It's a bold confrontation, a battle cry by the King of the universe against the so-called "prince of the sky." Elijah's message is an unpopular stand that will affect even the few faithful Israelites. And it's risky; Elijah's life is now in constant danger. He has declared himself and his God to be enemies of King Ahab's lord and master.

## Discuss

- There were other prophets in Israel during Ahab's reign; we're later told that Obadiah hid a hundred of them in a cave (18:4). Why does Elijah stand out in Scripture?

What makes him different than any other prophet of God?

_____

_____

_____

## A Long Wait: 1 Kings 17:2–16

The man who seemed to come out of the wilderness is sent back into it. God leads the prophet across the Jordan River to the edges of the kingdom, probably beyond Ahab's jurisdiction and certainly hidden from his view. Ravens bring him food—a role reversal for scavengers—and he drinks water from a brook. But when the brook dries up from the drought, God sends Elijah far away to another edge of the kingdom near Phoenicia, where a Gentile widow feeds him—a role reversal for a completely dependent member of society. The woman exercises great faith in feeding the prophet, as he asks for a portion of her last meal. But according to his promise, she never runs out of flour and oil for the duration of the drought. God favors her hospitality and faith with an endless supply.

## Discuss

- What does Elijah's experience tell you about God's willingness to provide for his people in lean times? Why do you think some people experience miraculous or unusual provision and some people don't?

_____

_____

_____

### A Lesson in Miracles: 1 Kings 17:17–24

Being a god of fertility, Baal is purported to govern the cycle of death and rebirth, just as the crops die and live with the seasons. So when the widow's son dies—when her only means of future support is taken from her—her own personal "war of the gods" begins. How could this happen while a prophet of Yahweh is staying with her? Why would God provide a miracle with her food supply yet not protect her son? Many consider it dangerous to be so close to a prophet, and now she sees why. She has benefited for a time, but her hospitality has come at a great cost. Is Baal punishing her for sheltering Yahweh's man? Or is Yahweh punishing her for her sins?

The woman brings her crisis to Elijah, and Elijah brings it to God. He spreads himself over the boy three times in a posture echoing an ancient healing incantation against demons, but he appeals to God alone. He imparts life back into the dead body, proving God's power over any life-stealing spirit. The widow's faith in Yahweh is restored.

## PROPHET TO PROPHET

In the biblical text, the widow and her son are never named. But a long-held rabbinic tradition asserts that the son Elijah revived was the prophet Jonah. It is believed that he grew up and joined the company of prophets who followed Elijah's successor, Elisha. Some even speculate that he was the unnamed prophet Elisha sent to anoint Jehu in 2 Kings 9:1–10. Though there is little biblical evidence for this tradition, it could easily fit the chronology of the prophets' lives. And if it's true, it makes for a dramatic picture: Elijah imparted more than life to the dead boy; he also imparted a prophetic spirit and calling.

**Discuss**

- How did the widow's perceptions of God change throughout this episode in Elijah's life? When everything seems to be going against you, are you more likely to see your circumstances as a sign of God's distance or an opportunity for him to act?

### A CASE STUDY

*Imagine:* Though your country certainly isn't perfect, it seems to be cruising along in relative prosperity. But an outspoken minister seizes a very public platform to declare God's judgment against the government—a judgment that would not only affect the leaders but would undermine the economy of the entire nation until the government repents. You're certainly in favor of more righteous leadership but not necessarily at the expense of everyone's welfare. That seems harsh and arbitrary. The next week, however, the once-stable economy plunges dramatically into a recession, and experts predict that it will last for years.

- Would you be more likely to see a connection between the minister's words and the faltering economy, or would you see the events as coincidental? Why?
- How are vocal preachers with harsh words generally perceived by society? How do you think Elijah was perceived in Israel?
- How well does this scenario fit your perceptions of God? Do you think God chastises governments today? Why or why not?

23

# Showdown

## 1 KINGS 18

Feodor wasn't naïve; he knew why most of his colleagues had disappeared. No one expressed opposition to Stalin's government for long without mysteriously fading into oblivion. Still, someone had to speak up. The fact that so many voices had been silenced made the need for voices that much greater. So Feodor, a newspaper editor already on thin ice with the government—he was sure they had been watching him—decided to make his voice as loud as possible, regardless of the consequences.

Moscow's citizens were shocked and probably amused one morning to read the open challenge on leaflets posted around town and on the front page of Feodor's paper. It was a daring gambit to all citizens of Stalinist society: a contest between prayer and science. Any two hopelessly terminally ill people—

the government's choice, to prove the contest wasn't rigged—would undergo separate treatments. One would receive the best medical resources available from the communist party's doctors, while the other would receive no treatment but Feodor's prayers. If neither patient survived, nothing would be proven. But if one lived and the other died, Feodor urged, all citizens should accept the results as vindication of the true worldview.

The stakes were high, but Feodor was convinced that his plan was inspired by God. How could the Stalinists refuse? If, as they believed, God didn't exist, then they had nothing to lose by accepting; they would appear cowardly if they declined. In fact, they could see the contest as an opportunity to publicly demonstrate that belief in God was mere superstition. And if God healed the patient whom Feodor prayed for, how could the government exile him? Communists certainly couldn't blame Feodor for the results; he had no power to heal anyone. But Feodor's opinions were now out in the open. If God didn't heal—if the contest produced no visible results—his life would essentially be over.

That fictional story captures at least some of the dynamics in Elijah's challenge to Ahab. The prophet set up a public opportunity for God and Baal to either show up or not, and Ahab couldn't refuse the proposal without looking scared. But if God didn't come through, Elijah's ministry would be over. He would be humiliated and killed on the spot, and Israel would continue to worship Baal.

Few believers are willing to put their faith to a public test like that—a winner-take-all contest for the hearts of human beings. Perhaps we don't know how God would respond when his people put his reputation on the line, so we avoid such awkward situations. But in Elijah's case, God relished the opportunity to demonstrate himself powerfully. He vindicated his servant in undeniable terms.

25

We may not find ourselves at the center of a high-profile showdown between God and secular society or Christianity and another religion, but our faith is frequently on display in much more subtle situations. Faith is put on the line daily. It involves risk, even the low-level kind in the details of routine life. If we're looking, we'll notice that God gives us plenty of opportunities to take a stand for what we believe. And those who are willing to take advantage of those opportunities will find him faithful.

**Confrontation: 1 Kings 18:1–19**

The three-year drought has taken its toll on Israel's landscape and Jezebel's nerves. She has relentlessly sought to eliminate the prophets of Yahweh—perhaps they have protested her Baal worship and posed a political threat, or maybe she assumes the drought is due to Baal's disfavor and seeks to eliminate those who have offended him. Regardless, a man named Obadiah, who is one of

## REPAIRER OF BROKEN ALTARS

Sacred mountains sometimes had altars at their summit. But more often shrines were placed near the foot of the mountain and only those with special privileges, such as priests, were allowed higher. That would explain why, after Elijah's victory over the priests of Baal, he and his servant ascended higher on Carmel to pray for rain (18:42) and even higher to watch for clouds over the sea (18:43). Their flaming altar had given them access to this ritual site. Regardless of where the altars were located, however, it seems that the priests of Baal already had one in place, while Elijah had to rebuild one that had previously been demolished (18:30). His effort to place stones upon ruins is a graphic physical picture of what he is doing spiritually: repairing the worship of Israel.

26

Ahab's top aides, has helped many true prophets escape her reach. As a prophetic advisor who oversees the palace, Obadiah must walk a thin line between God and the royal couple. He has hidden the prophets in caves and fed them from the palace stores.

So when Elijah appears to Obadiah and requests an audience with the king, the palace prophet is suspicious. Whether through compromise or righteous ingenuity, he has remained alive to this point. But reporting the whereabouts of the troubling prophet who is as elusive as the wind is risky. What if Elijah is blown away by the Spirit again? Ahab would vent his rage on Obadiah, and the refugees would have no provider.

But Elijah assures Obadiah that he will appear before the king, who jumps at the chance to confront his nemesis. The king and the prophet accuse each other of being Israel's downfall, and the latter offers a way to settle the dispute once and for all. A divine showdown will demonstrate who really has power over the skies and is worthy of the hearts of his people.

**Discuss**

- When is it appropriate to boldly confront someone over a spiritual matter? When is it appropriate to keep the peace? How can you discern the difference?

  _____

  _____

  _____

  _____

**Challenge: 1 Kings 18:20–40**

Whether for amusement or out of genuine spiritual concern, thousands of wishy-washy Israelites are drawn to Mount Carmel to witness the spectacle that has been advertised. Does it really matter what kind of altar one worships at? Isn't it a matter of personal preference? Many Israelites seem to think so, but Elijah takes the issue much more seriously than that. From his perspective, the future of monotheism is at stake. The people whom God had uniquely set apart for his purposes have almost completely blended in with the cultures around them. Whatever the outcome, for better or worse, this day will be a momentous event in the religious history of the world.

The 450 priests of Baal who were invited to the showdown come when Ahab summons them. The 400 priestesses of Asherah who were supported by the queen . . . well, they aren't mentioned for the rest of the chapter. Jezebel may have forbidden their participation in the contest on Mount Carmel. But the event goes on. Elijah sets the ground rules—an altar and a bull for each deity—and issues a challenge to the people. They must stop wavering (literally "hopping" or "limping") between two opinions and decide between Yahweh and Baal (18:21). The both/and approach to worship may be culturally acceptable, but the true God won't allow it. It's either/or. Pending the results of the showdown, the people agree to make a decisive choice.

The priests of Baal prepare their altar first and spend the better part of the day trying to ritually provoke their god. They invoke his name, appeal to his power, and circle the shrine, but there is no answer from the skies. At high noon—prime time for a god to light an altar on fire, if he has any intention of doing so—the prophet of Yahweh mocks them with their own fables of Baal's activities. Has he gone hunting? Must he be awakened? Is he meditating too deeply to notice their frantic pleas? There are Canaanite prayers for each scenario, but none are rousing the storm god, so greater measures are taken. The priests cut themselves and bleed to get Baal's attention.

Then they wait. Still no answer. No clouds or lightning strikes. Heaven is quiet.

Finally, the prophet gets his turn. In a symbolic statement about the spiritual unity of God's chosen people, Elijah uses twelve stones—one for each tribe of the true Israel—to rebuild an old altar to Yahweh that was presumably torn down by royal decree. And with twelve jars of water—a truly scarce commodity, if this isn't saltwater from the Mediterranean—he douses the altar. But God is not hindered by the alleged substance of Baal. Elijah prays that God would make himself known specifically as a God who wants people's hearts. Fire falls from heaven immediately, burns the offering, and even licks up the water.

The effects are powerful and immediate. With a phrase that echoes the meaning of Elijah's name, the people make their choice: "Yahweh is God," they chant again and again. The priests of Baal are slaughtered by the mob. God has won the showdown with startling ease.

## "THE GOD WHO ANSWERS BY FIRE"

Elijah's challenge leaves it to "the god who answers by fire" (18:24) to decide which deity is real. Why fire? As the storm god, Baal was thought to hold lightning in his hand. And in Israel's past, the true God had accepted the first sacrifice of Aaron's priesthood by consuming an offering with fire from heaven (Lev. 9:24). Whichever altar caught fire without human intervention would vindicate the entire worship system of either Elijah or the priests of Baal. If both sides had been praying for rain and then rain came, everyone would claim victory. But if Baal couldn't cast his lightning on a simple altar while God repeated his past acceptance of an offering, the source of the ensuing rain would be obvious.

**Discuss**

- Do you sometimes find yourself wavering between two opinions—that is, taking a both/and approach to God and his rivals in your heart rather than an either/or approach? If so, what do you think God might do to prompt you to make a clear commitment? How do you think you would respond if he did?

  _____

  _____

  _____

  _____

- Philosophers and theologians often argue that God won't prove himself to us—that he seeks those who will believe by faith alone. Why do you think God proved himself on Carmel? In what ways has he proved himself to you? In what ways has he not?

  _____

  _____

  _____

  _____

**Completion: 1 Kings 18:41–46**

Elijah ascends higher on the mountain and prays intensely. Seven times he sends his servant to see if the rain is coming, and finally a small cloud appears over the sea. The prophet knows God's timing has come. He warns the king to return to his palace before the heavy rains prevent safe passage. In spite of the day's drama, it's still a huge statement of faith. An impending deluge with no more evidence than a small cloud after three years of drought? But faith turns to sight quickly. The sky blackens, heavy rains come, and Ahab rides away to his queen.

Filled with the power of the Lord, the prophet runs before the chariot as though he holds a place of honor in the king's entourage. Does he assume Ahab's heart has changed? That the prophet and the king are now on the same side? Or is he simply making a statement as God's representative that the one true God now leads the king's chariot? It isn't clear, but Elijah stops short of the winter palace in Jezreel. The king is left to face his queen alone.

## Discuss

- Even though God had already said he would send rain (18:1), Elijah prayed intensely for rain to come and repeatedly sent his servant to look for the answer. Why do you think his prayers took time and persistence? In the absence of an answer, how can we know when God wants us to keep praying persistently and when he has said no?

_____

_____

_____

_____

## A Case Study

_Imagine:_ You were raised with a certain set of beliefs, and you've stuck with them faithfully all your life. Not only have you wholeheartedly believed, but you've also been trained to be an authority in your faith. You teach and lead others. You pray a lot and

31

often receive answers. But now a new religious movement has risen up and challenged your convictions. Its members receive greater answers to their prayers and experience more miracles. Their faith seems to be accompanied by an undeniable divine power, and you aren't sure how to explain that.

- How dramatically would one religion have to be proven in order for you to abandon what you've always believed and embrace it? Would anything convince you to give up your long-held beliefs?

- How do you think Ahab interpreted the events on Mount Carmel? If you had been one of the prophets of Baal, how would you have interpreted them?

- Paul wrote that "my message and my preaching were not with wise and persuasive words, but with a demonstration of the Spirit's power" (1 Cor. 2:4) and that "the king-dom of God is not a matter of talk but of power" (1 Cor. 4:20). How did this principle play out in Israel during the drought and at Mount Carmel? How do you think it plays out today?

# A Season of Discontent

## 1 KINGS 19, 21

Michael started out with zeal, but it didn't take long for him to realize that the Christian life isn't exactly a bed of roses. Half of his family thought he was nuts for becoming "a Jesus fanatic"— that's how they labeled his faith. And now they thought he was nuts for hanging onto it. They didn't exactly say "I told you so," but after losing his job, getting deeper into debt, struggling with ongoing tension in his marriage, and spending three weeks in the hospital after a nasty car accident, it was obvious to everyone that Michael's faith hadn't made his problems go away. In fact, some of his problems seemed to get worse after he believed. And now, though he would never admit it to his skeptical family members, he was becoming as disillusioned with Christians as his family had always been. Were Christians really a "new creation"? Was he? Maybe God didn't have as wonderful a plan for his life as he had thought.

Discouragement amid life's struggles is normal for any human being but especially for those who hope that the Holy Spirit's presence in their life might make all roads smooth. And when faith encounters disappointment too persistently or too deeply, discouragement can easily turn into disillusionment. So it was with Elijah, who had just experienced a great victory at the climax of his ministry. But the victory didn't accomplish all he had hoped. He had spent himself completely on a task that reaped only part of the fruit he expected. With nothing left to give, he sank into disillusionment.

Most people can relate to that, at least at some moments in their lives. Many feel like giving up, and some even pray Elijah's prayer: "Take my life." Christians are not immune from those thoughts. Even if we don't experience them ourselves, we come into contact daily with people who do. In the various trials of life, we and those around us are reminded of what it's like to be wounded and broken.

God understands the discouraging moments in our lives. He even braces us for them. Peter told his readers not to be surprised at the painful trials they were facing (1 Peter 4:12), and John told his readers not to be surprised if the world hated them (1 John 3:13). That's because a life of faith that comes with no trials is a contradiction. It doesn't exist. Those who believe in God and his kingdom will experience conflict and hardships in this world. But they will also experience God's grace, his strength, and his words of encouragement. In the moments of our greatest disappointments, he comes to us with mercy.

## Vengeance: 1 Kings 19:1–5

The queen is furious. She doesn't repent of her idolatry, even after Ahab fills her in on all the details of the day's events. God

## A DRY PLACE

Elijah spent three years in a drought that he had proclaimed, then fled to the Judean wilderness to get away from Jezebel. From there, he traveled to Mount Sinai—or, as it's typically called in Deuteronomy, Mount Horeb, which means "desolate" or "dry place." It's a fitting picture not only for the nature of his ministry but also for how he feels spiritually after the showdown on Carmel. His ministry has been relatively dry, and his soul is wrestling with an even greater sense of drought. But just as God provided for his physical needs by the brook, with the ravens, and at the home of the widow, he now provides for the prophet's spiritual needs. God meets Elijah—and us—even in the driest places in life.

won the hearts of the people who happened to be at Carmel—a significant number, in fact—but the national repentance Elijah hoped for, the ultimate goal of the long and painful drought, never materialized. No, Jezebel hardens her heart even further, and Ahab seems to have no option but to comply. The worship of Baal and Asherah is still the state religion. This is not how it was supposed to turn out.

The fact that the prophet-killing queen could increase her rage in spite of God's winning such a decisive victory is frightening. If the display of power on Carmel didn't change hearts, what would? And if Jezebel had succeeded in slaughtering so many other prophets of Yahweh, what will stop her from slaughtering the one she wants most—the one who is no longer hidden from view, as he had been for three long years? Now out in the open and apparently vulnerable to royal power, Elijah is gripped with fear. He runs to the nearest city in the southern kingdom and leaves his servant there. Then he walks a day's journey into the wilderness and sits down under a tree.

Exhausted and depressed, Elijah asks God to take his life and lies down to die.

**Discuss**

- How can someone who just experienced the overwhelming power of God become as discouraged as Elijah did?

  _____

  _____

  _____

  _____

- Have you experienced a letdown after a major life event? If so, what do you think caused it? Could your discouragement have been avoided if you had managed your expectations differently?

  _____

  _____

  _____

  _____

**Visitation: 1 Kings 19:6–21**

An angel ministers to Elijah, and the prophet is sustained with the same food once given to him by the widow. But the second time the angel brings sustenance, it isn't for recovery. It's preparation for a journey. Elijah is about to be taken back to Israel's roots in a series of events that parallels the great prophet Moses long before him: a journey through the wilderness, a period of forty days and nights, a visitation from God at Mount Sinai, a cleft in the rock when God's power passes by. Mount Sinai is the site where Moses saw the burning bush, where the blessings

## QUEEN OF WICKEDNESS

Jezebel didn't just steal one man's property via an illegitimate trial and murder. She stole an entire family's piece of the Promised Land. The Naboth incident is a graphic picture of the idolatrous queen as a thief of Israel's inheritance—both literally and figuratively—and therefore a representative of all that would distract God's chosen people from their destiny. The brutal demise of this queen of "idolatry and witchcraft" is recorded in 2 Kings 9, but her reputation became even more legendary throughout history. She shows up in Revelation 2:20–23 as a symbol of false prophecy, false worship, and sinful seduction. Throughout history, she has become a symbol of those who tempt and manipulate godly people.

and curses of Deuteronomy were first pronounced, where God made his covenant with his chosen people, and where fire first fell from heaven onto Aaron's altar to confirm his priesthood (Lev. 9:24). Even among the Israelites who have worshiped Baal, it's still known as a place where the thunder and lightning of God's presence was made manifest. And it's where Elijah must encounter the God he has served.

The prophet declares his own faithfulness—and how his faithfulness has isolated him from his people. "I alone am left," he says, and if he's speaking of prophets who have taken a stand and survived, he may be right. But he is not the only person in Israel who has remained faithful to God. He is not as alone as he thinks.

Like Moses, Elijah is told to find shelter in a cave on the mountain—literally *the* cave, as in the *same one*. Like Moses, he witnesses the presence of God passing by. A series of violent displays shows what God's power is like: a terrifying wind rips into the mountain and shatters rocks while the prophet clings to safety; an earthquake shakes the foundation of the mountain itself; fire falls from heaven and rages around the cave. But those displays are the power of the Lord, not his presence. When the unnerving tumult ceases, an eerie silence remains. Some call it a "still, small voice" or a "gentle whisper," but it's literally a "very thin stillness"—a "hear a pin drop" kind of hush. That's where the weight of God's presence is, and that's where Elijah comes face-to-face with his disappointments.

God addresses the prophet's weariness with a word of encouragement—7,000 Israelites still have not bowed to Baal—and with a plan to anoint his successor. All of God's words give some sort of assurance that he has not forsaken Israel, he still has plans for his people, and Elijah's ministry has been a part of those plans. The prophet gets up, goes back to Israel, finds the man who will succeed him, and imparts his calling to the next generation.

### Discuss

- Why do you think God took Elijah to Mount Sinai to sort things out?

  _____

  _____

  _____

  _____

- To what degree do you wrestle with discouragement? In what specific ways did God deal with Elijah's disappointment and fear? How does he normally deal with yours?

  _____

  _____

  _____

  _____

## Verdict: 1 Kings 21

### *Focus: 1 Kings 21:17–29*

Ahab covets a vineyard next to his winter palace in Jezreel, so he asks the owner, Naboth, to sell it to him or trade him for it. It isn't an unreasonable request—selling one's land is permissible under God's law, so Naboth is certainly allowed by God to consider his options. But a family's property is its piece of Israel's promise from God, and vineyards are an inheritance cultivated over many generations. Naboth declines, and the king is frustrated.

Jezebel doesn't understand why a king shouldn't claim whatever land he wants, so she concocts a plan. She finds two wicked witnesses to testify that Naboth is guilty of capital crimes he never committed: blasphemy against God and treason against the king. He is summarily executed, and Ahab takes his land.

God hates injustice, and he commissions Elijah to declare Ahab's guilt. The king and queen—the authorities established by God to uphold justice in the land—have committed an outrageous wrong, breaking at least four of the Ten Commandments (coveting, bearing false witness, stealing, and murder) in addition to the idolatry they have long practiced. Because of such blatant rebellion, God will bring disaster on the king, the queen, and their entire dynasty. For once, Ahab believes Elijah's words—how could the prophet have known of the plot unless it had been divinely revealed to him?—and he is grieved. He demonstrates remorse (though not enough to give the vineyard back to Naboth's family). Judgment will still come—he and Jezebel will both die rather brutal deaths—but disaster won't fall on the kingdom until the next generation.

**Discuss**

- Knowing God's passion for justice, what role do you think Christians should have in speaking out against social injustice? Why do you think many Christians don't?

_____

_____

_____

### A Case Study

*Imagine:* You've been serving God with all your heart for years. But now you've reached a point of exhaustion; frankly, you wonder if your service has been worth the effort. You've seen some fruit, but not as much as you hoped for. At the end of your rope, in a moment of deep discouragement, you vent your frustration to God. Why hasn't he given you more support? Why aren't you soaring on wings of eagles, as he promised? Why does life have to be so hard? You ask him all the difficult questions. And in the silence you hear his voice: "I have chosen someone to replace you ..."

- Is God's promise to provide someone to carry on your mission a comfort to you or an offense? Are you relieved that there will be help or insulted that he thinks your work is done?
- How do you think Elijah felt about God hearing his complaints and then immediately naming his successor? How do you think God intended it?
- Why do you think burnout occurs among Christians— people who are filled with and empowered by God's Spirit? How can we prevent it? How should we deal with burnout when we face it?

# Succession

## 2 KINGS 1–2

Deep inside the human heart is a hunger for the supernatural. Somehow we know there's more to life than what we can see. Even those who deny the possibility of miracles hope for one in a crisis.

That yearning plays out in different ways for different people. As Christians, most of us are driven to our knees to pray for God's intervention, confident he has the ability to overcome an impossibility against all odds. Some end up following charlatans, blinded by their hope that someone with a semblance of godliness has finally tapped into supernatural power. Others just resign themselves to "reality," assuming that while God *can* do miracles, he probably won't. We're left with a lot of theology about what God normally does (or doesn't do) and why he normally does it (or not), and nearly everyone has his or her own take on the issue. But apart from all the speculations and convictions, the fact remains that God has placed this longing within us, and so we reach upward for a power greater than ourselves.

Elisha hungered for the spirit that operated in Elijah, so much so that he asked for a double-sized piece of it. And surely he knew the ramifications—that Elijah's spirit couldn't be broken up and distributed in pieces; that the supernatural gifts would come as a package deal with the hardships and the opposition; that dramatic miracles are not who God is, but what he sometimes chooses to do; that in spite of all the wind and fire and earthquakes, the presence of God is in the stillness. Even so, Elisha wanted the package. Those who really hunger for God usually do. They want him at all costs.

## THE MESSAGE IN THE NAMES

Elijah's name means "Yahweh is God"—a strong message that demands repentance and complete faithfulness. But he is followed by a prophet whose name means "God saves" or "God is salvation"—a grace-filled message for those who fall short. The dynamic is profound enough in Elijah and Elisha, but consider the bigger scriptural pattern. The lawgiver Moses was followed by a successor named Yehoshua (Joshua)—"God saves." And John the Baptist, who came in the spirit of Elijah, was followed by a Messiah with the same name—Yeshua (Jesus), or "God saves." The two prophets in 1–2 Kings are like a snapshot in the middle of the Old Testament that points back to the Promised Land and forward to the Messiah's kingdom. That picture makes the journey of 2 Kings 2 even more meaningful. As though God were saying "Let's start over," the two men leave the Promised Land together, the messenger of repentance ascends in the same place where Moses died and John would later baptize, and then "God saves" walks back across the Jordan into the land.

In 2 Kings 2, the time came for Elijah to pass the prophetic baton to Elisha. We'll see how Elijah did his best to discourage Elisha's hunger, knowing that true hunger would not comply with a simple rebuff. Elisha didn't just want a double portion of Elijah's spirit, he wanted God. And God granted both prophets yet another display of his power, the greatest either of them had yet seen. Because they had their hearts set on God himself, regardless of the cost, God showed them another picture of his glory.

God's desire for each of us is that we hunger for him—not just for his power, not just for his favors, not just for his miracles, but for him. When we long for him more than for what he can give us, we tend to see his gifts more frequently. He opens his hands generously to those who seek his heart.

## Mission Accomplished: 2 Kings 2:1–10

Ahab has died, and his son Ahaziah is now king. Like his father, Ahaziah is a Baal worshiper. And, like his father, he has contentious encounters with the outspoken prophet Elijah. But eventually the time comes for Elijah to depart. His mission to the kings of Israel is over.

The prophet's imminent departure seems to be no secret. He knows it, Elisha knows it, even an entire company of prophets knows it. As Elijah and Elisha are traveling from Gilgal to Bethel, the older prophet urges his protégé to let him go on alone. No, replies Elisha. He will not leave his mentor. The exchange is repeated again on the way to Jericho, and again on the way to the Jordan River. The pair takes virtually the reverse route out of the Promised Land from what Joshua and the Israelites used to enter it centuries before. They cross the river—supernaturally, just like Joshua did—and arrive very nearly at the place where Moses completed his mission and died.

"What can I do for you before I am taken from you?" Elijah asks Elisha. Like a firstborn son who, according to the law of Moses, receives a double share of his father's inheritance, the younger prophet asks for a double portion of Elijah's spirit. The teacher reminds his student how hard the prophetic calling is; a double portion is a heavy burden. But Elisha wants it anyway. And Elijah tells him how to recognize whether his request has been granted. If he can keep his eyes on the master, the double portion is his.

### Discuss

- If you could receive a direct impartation from a mentor or respected leader, what spiritual gift or calling would you ask for? Why? What costs do you think would accompany the benefits?

  _____

  _____

  _____

  _____

### Miraculous Ascent: 2 Kings 2:11–18

Suddenly, fire falls from heaven again—this time in the form of a horse-drawn chariot that separates the two men. Elisha looks across to the other side of the chariot and sees Elijah ascending to heaven in a whirlwind. He cries out in the chaotic scene, and in a moment his master is gone.

The master's coat remains, however, and Elisha picks up the symbol of his calling. Has he received the double portion he asked for? He saw Elijah ascend—that was the sign—and now he holds his cloak. "Where now is the LORD, the God of

## A FAMILIAR CALLING

When Elijah threw his cloak over Elisha (1 Kings 19:19)—a symbolic gesture with clear implications—the younger prophet was plowing in a field and asked to go say good-bye to his family. Centuries later, when a would-be follower of Jesus asked to go say good-bye to his family first, Jesus echoed Elisha's calling with these words: "No one who puts his hand to the plow and looks back is fit for service in the kingdom of God" (Luke 9:62). Was it a rebuke of this revered prophet's response? Probably not—after all, Elisha cut ties with his past by slaughtering his oxen and burning his plow. But it was at least a statement about the seriousness of following Jesus. Those in the kingdom of God need to have a sense of commitment as strong or stronger than Elisha's.

Elijah?" he asks, striking the river with the garment. The waters divide, just as they had divided for Elijah when they came across earlier in the day and just as they had divided for Joshua after his mentor, Moses, died.

The company of prophets, who had followed to the edge of the river but not crossed over, has a hard time believing Elisha's story when he returns. A chariot of fire? Ascending in a whirl-wind? They knew Elijah was going to be taken from them, but perhaps they expected a normal death. Or maybe, they suggest hopefully, the Spirit set him back down again somewhere. They insist on sending out search parties, but they find nothing. The prophet whom Obadiah once suspected of being as elusive as the wind is just as mysterious in his final departure.

**Discuss**

- Elijah's role in Israel's kingdom ended, but his mission was carried on by a successor chosen by God. How important is it to you to be part of a larger purpose that will last longer than your lifetime? How intentional are you about fitting into God's plan and establishing a lasting legacy?

_____

_____

_____

_____

## A CASE STUDY

*Imagine:* You're sitting around with your friends and talking about how much you want your life to count for something in eternity—how you want God to use you for his purposes. Suddenly, a hairy, odd-looking man dressed in leather garments and filling the room with a somewhat unpleasant odor appears out of thin air and declares himself to be Elijah. He is wildly passionate about God and delighted that you want to serve—"not many people do," he laments. If you're willing, he can supernaturally impart his gifts and calling to you on the spot. But he sternly warns you that being used by God is a serious and heavy task. The demands are relentless, the oppression—both internal and external—can be severe, and you may go through periods of being extremely lonely, frustrated, and discouraged. The rewards, however, are amazing and everlasting. Sure, you may lose your life, but you will gain so much more.

- How readily would you take up this strange, hairy prophet on his offer to impart his gifts and calling to you? Would you accept immediately, or would you tell him you'd have to think about it?

- What would you think if someone in your circle of friends said, "Sure—but may I have two helpings of whatever you have, hardships and all?"
- In what sense is this offer already on the table for all Christians? In your opinion, how willing are most people to really take God up on it? Why?

# Legacy

Eli loved this moment of Passover. The fourth cup of the Seder meal had just been poured and, as the youngest child in the family, he got to go open the front door for Elijah—the prophet for whom he was named. Everyone would stand and sing, "*Eliyahu hanavi, Eliyahu hatishbi . . .*" And he was old enough to understand the words now: "Elijah the prophet, Elijah the Tishbite, Elijah of Gilead, come quickly in our day. Come to us, Messiah, son of David."

Eli wondered if Elijah really ever came through the front door—if he invisibly entered, sat in the empty chair reserved for him, and drank from the cup of wine specially poured for him. Much of Passover seemed mysterious, but the thought of Elijah visiting was especially so. He was a welcome guest in any Jewish home. And one day when he comes in the flesh . . . well, that will mean only one thing: Messiah is on his way.

That's the scene in many Jewish homes at Passover—the intangible presence of Elijah invited in and honored as a symbol of righteousness and the Messianic kingdom. Perhaps more than any other figure in Hebrew Scripture apart from Abraham and Moses, Elijah is revered as a picture of restoration. And the New Testament has a lot to say about him too. He represents hope for all who desire God's kingdom to come.

Ultimately, that's what we all long for—the kingdom to come. We want a world full of true worship, justice, and faithfulness. We want hearts to be turned back to God and for God to act powerfully on our behalf. We yearn for a time of fullness. According to Scripture, that time will come.

## A Symbol of Things to Come: Malachi 4:5–6

The last two verses of the Hebrew prophetic Scriptures point to the prophet who never died. Elijah will come again, Malachi says, before the "great and dreadful day of the LORD." But what does that

## MYSTERIOUS ENDINGS

Nearly all biblical heroes, even the most revered among them, died normal deaths. But the few exceptions are notable. Enoch walked with God, and then God "took him away" (Gen. 5:24). Moses died on Mount Nebo, but Deuteronomy 34:6 indicates that the Lord himself buried him and no one ever knew where the grave was—hence the speculation in Jewish writings before the time of Jesus that Moses's body mysteriously disappeared and was disputed by angels (see Jude 1:9). Elijah's ascension is most dramatic, but also most clearly witnessed. So if human beings are appointed to die once (Heb. 9:27), what is to be said of the two Old Testament characters who never did? Some have speculated that they are the two witnesses who minister and are killed in Revelation 11—though the powers given them in 11:6 seem to suggest Moses and Elijah rather than Enoch and Elijah. Regardless, the witnesses have "power to shut up the sky so that it will not rain during the time they are prophesying"—which, not surprisingly, is 1,260 days, or three and a half years.

mean? Before final judgment? That's what "the day of the Lord" usually refers to. Before the Messiah comes? That's how Jewish tradition has usually interpreted the prophecy. Both? Many people see the day of the Lord and the Messiah's return as simultaneous events. Regardless, Elijah comes with a specific mission: to turn the hearts of fathers and sons back toward one another.

Elijah inhabits Jewish expectations in many ways. As we've seen, he represents hope for ultimate deliverance at each Passover. At the end of each Yom Kippur (Day of Atonement) service, his message is repeated seven times: "The Lord alone is God." As a preacher of righteousness, he will one day settle all disputed interpretations of the Talmud. As a defender of Israel's covenant, he is said to be present at every covenant circumcision. As the one who inhabits the "chair of Elijah" at each circumcision, he will be able to inform all men of their true genealogy and tribal identity. In nearly every respect, he is considered a sign of the culmination of God's plan.

**Discuss**

- What characteristics of God's kingdom do you most look forward to? In what ways did Elijah's ministry in 1–2 Kings represent those characteristics?

  _____

  _____

  _____

**A Once and Future Prophet: Matthew 17:1–13**

Jesus took three of his disciples up on a mountain, and suddenly his appearance changed. Two figures from the Hebrew Scriptures—Moses and Elijah, pictures of the law and the prophets—joined him and spoke with him. But the representatives of the law and the prophets suddenly disappeared, and God's voice declared Jesus to be the beloved Son. Similar to what God had demonstrated on another mountain long ago, the glory of his presence wasn't in a sensational manifestation—the supernatural appearance of Moses and Elijah. It was in the subtler moments of life—in the Teacher whom the disciples had been talking to every day.

The experience on the mountain raised a lot of questions for the disciples, one of which focused on the Jewish expectations of Elijah's return. If the Son of Man is with us, they reasoned, why hasn't Elijah come first as the sages say he will? Jesus's answer is enigmatic: Elijah will come and restore all things, he tells them. He uses the future tense and describes a ministry no one has fulfilled before the Son's first coming. But in another sense, Elijah has already come, he says. John baptized in the spirit of Elijah as a forerunner for the Messiah. So Jesus is intentionally ambiguous: Elijah has come, and Elijah will come.

## Discuss

- What similarities do you see between Elijah and John the Baptist? What differences do you see?

  _____

  _____

  _____

- Do you think Jesus's statement about Elijah restoring all things means that the Old Testament Elijah will come again before Jesus returns? Why or why not?

  _____

  _____

  _____

**A Powerful Example: James 5:17–18**

"Elijah was a man just like us." At least that's what James says (5:17), though we may notice quite a few differences between the bold prophet and our own lifestyles. Still, his point is clear: with a fallen human nature, a man dedicated to God prayed powerfully enough that God shut the skies for over three years and then opened them again. And James encourages us to see Elijah not as an exception but as an example. In other words, in our prayer life we can have the prophet's mantle too.

**Discuss**

- According to James, Elijah is proof of the power of prayer. To what degree do you relate to this example? Does it encourage you to pray bolder prayers? Why or why not?

  _____

  _____

  _____

## A SACRED SITE

Archaeologists believe they have found Bethany-beyond-Jordan, the wilderness home of John the Baptist (John 1:28), and the location is loaded with symbolism. It's across the Jordan River from Jericho—exactly where Scripture describes both the death of Moses and the ascension of Elijah. Not only are these three characters tied together by the way the Bible overlaps their ministry roles, they are united in geography as well, as if God wanted to make it clear that Elijah carried on Moses's ministry and John carried on Elijah's. And Scripture says that all three point directly to the Messiah.

## A CASE STUDY

*Imagine:* You've experienced answers to prayer before but never like this. Suddenly, every request that comes out of your mouth when you talk with God is fulfilled within days, sometimes even hours. It's almost scary how effective your prayers have become, as though the power of the universe is in your hands to wield however you choose. Your words have the ability to change the course of people's lives. And the power seems to be the same whether you're praying for situations close to you or on a global scale. Your words can heal bodies, thwart or fulfill plans, secure jobs, repair relationships, impact nations, and even change weather patterns. Not even the sky is the limit.

- With such power seemingly at your fingertips, how would you begin to prioritize your prayers? What situations would make the top of your list? Which ones would fall toward the bottom?
- Why do you think Elijah prayed for a drought to prompt repentance rather than simply praying that people would repent?
- In what sense is this power in prayer the promise of Scripture? Do you think Christians should experience such dramatic answers regularly? Why or why not?

# Conclusion

Elisha once asked a question echoed by many throughout the centuries, especially in spiritually dry times: "Where is the God of Elijah?" It's a legitimate question. If God showed up so powerfully in one generation, why wouldn't he do so in another? Why would he confront Ahab and Jezebel through Elijah while letting other wicked kings in other countries run their course unopposed? Or has he, in fact, sent Elijah-like prophets into other kingdoms whose stories we do not know? Perhaps we've run into some of them without recognizing them—or worse, were offended by them. Maybe we're trying to recognize the God of Elijah by his power rather than by his correction. It's entirely possible that in our search for the God of Elijah, we don't know what we're looking for.

That's because, at least in part, Elijah himself was an enigma—a brash, politically incorrect, blunt instrument of God's voice. He experienced God's blessing and administered God's justice. He experienced resounding spiritual victories, yet he still wandered the wilderness in defeat. He learned how to recognize the still, small voice of God's presence, yet he was taken to heaven in a spectacular display. At times, he seemed to be the sanest man in Israel and at other times, to be the most unstable. His words were shocking, pointed, and often considered rude, yet he spoke for God. He was—and is—hard to figure out.

Elijah lived a difficult life. That's because he was called to make a huge difference in a status-quo world. The judgments he spoke—that God decreed through him—would be hard on the people of Israel, some of whom had no idea why rain didn't fall for three and half years and who had an extremely difficult time finding food and water. He endured the rage of a wicked government, apparently wondering how God could seem to support him one minute and abandon him the next. And after his meltdown at Sinai, he never seemed the same again. Before his crisis, he had proclaimed judgment unless people repented; afterward, only judgment. We see no hint of enthusiasm in his life after Sinai. He had spent himself on God in extremely trying times.

Perhaps that's why Elisha's question isn't the best one to be asking in our generation. Where is the God of Elijah? He's still calling his people to abandon divided hearts and serve him faithfully, to stop wavering between truth and compromise, to go back to the beginning and remember the faith we were called to live. Maybe he's waiting for his people to place both feet firmly in his kingdom, regardless of the cost, and live with Elijah's bold, bare commitment. Perhaps the real question isn't "Where is the God of Elijah?" but "Where are the Elijahs of God?"

# Leader's Notes

## Session 1

*A Case Study.* There are quite a few similarities between this situation and the way most cultures express their religious beliefs. In discussing these questions, it may be important to address the fact that ancient Israel had a unique role in God's plan. His way of dealing with Israel's apostasy is probably different than how he would deal with religious pluralism in a democracy, for example. But his attitude toward those who have forsaken his Word might still be the same. For the sake of your discussion, consider focusing on a comparison not between Israel and a modern society but between Israel and the church.

## Session 3

*1 Kings 18:1–19, discussion questions.* The Christian's responsibility to "speak the truth in love" is at the heart of these questions. Group members may have no trouble discussing the difficulties involved with this, but if the conversation doesn't get off the ground, try mentioning some specific situations. Do you boldly confront someone over immoral behavior? Over unbiblical beliefs? When they are hurting themselves, or only when their decisions and behavior are harming other people? How serious does their error have to be before confrontation becomes necessary? Raising questions like these will help highlight the difficulty in deciding when and how to confront.

*1 Kings 18:41–46, discussion questions.* Some people see God's promises as an invitation to pray and believe, while others see them as a statement of destiny or fate. How we view his promises will determine how we pray—how long we persist, when we give up, when we assume that his silence means "no." Try to draw out as many perspectives on this issue as you can, affirming both the certainty of God's promises and the need for us to believe and receive them.

## Session 6

*Matthew 17:1–13, first discussion question.* Jesus compared John the Baptist with Elijah and said that John fulfilled at least part of the prophecy of Elijah's return. In discussing the similarities between them, you'll most likely focus on things such as their common message of repentance, their wilderness lifestyle, and their predictions of judgment against their contemporary political and religious leaders. But there are also significant differences. In contrast to Elijah, John did no miracles, was brutally executed, and constantly pointed to someone greater than himself still to come.

# Bibliography

Auld, A. Graeme. *I & II Kings.* Louisville: Westminster John Knox Press, 1986.

Berlin, Adele, Marc Zvi Brettler, and Michael Fishbane, eds. *The Jewish Study Bible.* Oxford and New York: Oxford University Press, 2004.

Elman, Yaakov. *The Living Nach: Early Prophets.* New York: Moznaim Publishing Company, 1994.

Kaiser, Walter C., Jr., and Duane Garrett, eds. *Archaeological Study Bible.* Grand Rapids: Zondervan, 2006.

*Mikraoth Geoloth: Kings I.* Brooklyn, NY: The Judaica Press, 1980.

Scherman, Nosson. *The Prophets: Kings.* Brooklyn, NY: Mesorah Publications, 2006.

Telushkin, Joseph. *Biblical Literacy: The Most Important People, Events, and Ideas of the Hebrew Bible.* New York: William Morrow, 1997.

Walton, John H., Victor H. Matthews, and Mark W. Chavalas. *The IVP Bible Background Commentary: Old Testament.* Downers Grove, IL: InterVarsity Press, 2000.

**WALK THRU** the **BIBLE**®

# Helping people everywhere live God's Word

For more than three decades, Walk Thru the Bible has created discipleship materials and cultivated leadership networks that together are reaching millions of people through live seminars, print publications, audiovisual curricula, and the Internet. Known for innovative methods and high-quality resources, we serve the whole body of Christ across denominational, cultural, and national lines. Through our strong and cooperative international partnerships, we are strategically positioned to address the church's greatest need: developing mature, committed, and spiritually reproducing believers.

Walk Thru the Bible communicates the truths of God's Word in a way that makes the Bible readily accessible to anyone. We are committed to developing user-friendly resources that are Bible centered, of excellent quality, life changing for individuals, and catalytic for churches, ministries, and movements; and we are committed to maintaining our global reach through strategic partnerships while adhering to the highest levels of integrity in all we do.

Walk Thru the Bible partners with the local church worldwide to fulfill its mission, helping people "walk thru" the Bible with greater clarity and understanding. Live seminars and small group curricula are taught in over 45 languages by more than 80,000 people in more than 70 countries, and more than 100 million devotionals have been packaged into daily magazines, books, and other publications that reach over five million people each year.

Walk Thru the Bible
4201 North Peachtree Road
Atlanta, GA 30341-1207
770-458-9300
www.walkthru.org

# Read the entire Bible in one year, thanks to the systematic reading plan in the bestselling **Daily Walk** devotional.

The **Daily Walk** devotional magazine includes book introductions, charts outlining book and chapter themes, and background information on each day's reading. Insightful observations shed light on the culture, the history, and the context of passages. Each daily reading is loaded with helpful applications that enable you to apply biblical truth to your life. Readers are sure to find the time they spend in the Bible more productive and rewarding than ever before.

Ideal for church-wide or group Bible study, bulk subscriptions to **Daily Walk** offering significant savings can be purchased online at www.walkthru.org. Discounted individual subscriptions are also available online.